NEW MONTH

BRAIN DUMP

....

....

....

....

....

....

....

....

....

....

....

....

....

....

....

Philippians 4:13

I can do all things through Christ who strengthens me.

I0135836

MONTHLY PLANNER

Month _____

M	T	W	T	F	S	S

Psalm 139:14

I praise you because I am fearfully and wonderfully made;
your works are wonderful,
I know that full well.

Monthly Budget

Income		
Income-1		
Income-2		
Other Income		
	Total Income	

Expenses	
Month	
Budget	

Bill To Be Paid	Due Date	Amount	Paid	Notes
	Total			

Monthly Summary		
Total Income	Total Expenses	Difference

Notes

3

Savings Goal

GOAL:	DATE	AMOUNT
SAVINGS:		
DEADLINE:		

TOTAL:

Week of: _____

Weekly Planner

This Week's Goal:

Important Tasks

Appointments

To Do List

Proverbs 16:9
The heart of man plans his way, but the Lord
establishes his steps.

Weekly Goals

Day	Goals	Action Steps
Mon		
Tue		
Wed		
Thu		
Fri		
Sat		

GRATITUDE REMINDER

- I am thankful for

- I am grateful for

- Notes

Psalm 100:4-5
Enter his gates with thanksgiving
and his courts with praise;
give thanks to him and praise his
name.
For the Lord is good and his love
endures forever;
his faithfulness continues through all
generations.

MY WEEKLY PRAYER

_____
_____
_____
_____
_____
_____
_____
_____
_____
_____
_____
_____
_____
_____

SCRIPTURE OF THE WEEK

PRAYER REQUEST

_____
_____
_____
_____
_____
_____
_____
_____
_____
_____
_____
_____
_____
_____

Week of: _____

Weekly Planner

To Do List

This Week's Goal:

Important Tasks

Appointments

Proverbs 16:9
The heart of man plans his way, but the Lord
establishes his steps.

Weekly Goals

Day	Goals	Action Steps
Mon		
Tue		
Wed		
Thu		
Fri		
Sat		

GRATITUDE REMINDER

- **I am thankful for**

- **I am grateful for**

- **Notes**

Psalm 100:4-5
Enter his gates with thanksgiving
and his courts with praise;
give thanks to him and praise his
name.
For the Lord is good and his love
endures forever;
his faithfulness continues through all
generations.

MY WEEKLY PRAYER

SCRIPTURE OF THE WEEK

PRAYER REQUEST

Week of: _____

Weekly Planner

To Do List

This Week's Goal:

Important Tasks

Appointments

Proverbs 16:9
The heart of man plans his way, but the Lord
establishes his steps.

Weekly Goals

Day	Goals	Action Steps
Mon		
Tue		
Wed		
Thu		
Fri		
Sat		

GRATITUDE REMINDER

- I am thankful for

  _____
  _____
  _____

- I am grateful for

  _____
  _____
  _____

- Notes

Psalm 100:4-5
Enter his gates with thanksgiving
and his courts with praise;
give thanks to him and praise his
name.
For the Lord is good and his love
endures forever;
his faithfulness continues through all
generations.

MY WEEKLY PRAYER

_____
_____
_____
_____
_____
_____
_____
_____
_____
_____
_____
_____
_____

SCRIPTURE OF THE WEEK

PRAYER REQUEST

_____
_____
_____
_____
_____
_____
_____
_____
_____
_____
_____
_____

Week of: _____

Weekly Planner

This Week's Goal:

To Do List

Important Tasks

Appointments

Proverbs 16:9
The heart of man plans his way, but the Lord
establishes his steps.

Weekly Goals

Day	Goals	Action Steps
Mon		
Tue		
Wed		
Thu		
Fri		
Sat		

GRATITUDE REMINDER

- I am thankful for

- I am grateful for

- Notes

Psalm 100:4-5
Enter his gates with thanksgiving
and his courts with praise;
give thanks to him and praise his
name.
For the Lord is good and his love
endures forever;
his faithfulness continues through all
generations.

MY WEEKLY PRAYER

SCRIPTURE OF THE WEEK

PRAYER REQUEST

Personal Reflection

Month:

BAD HABITS I NEED TO STOP

THINGS I REGRETTED NOT DOING

THINGS I LEARNED THIS MONTH

HOW TO BE A BETTER VERSION OF ME

30 DAY
Self-Care Challenge

DAY 1	DAY 2	DAY 3	DAY 4	DAY 5
Start a gratitude journal	Learn to meditate	Spend the day social media free	Call someone you love	Take a 15 minute walk outdoors

DAY 6	DAY 7	DAY 8	DAY 9	DAY 10
Listen to a podcast	Learn to cook a new recipe	Stretch for 10-15 minutes	Listen to your favorite song	Practice deep breathing

DAY 11	DAY 12	DAY 13	DAY 14	DAY 15
Try a free online workout	Read a book for 15 minutes	Write a list of short-term goals	De-clutter a room or desk	Go to bed 30 minutes earlier

DAY 16	DAY 17	DAY 18	DAY 19	DAY 20
Have a game night	Wake up 15 minutes earlier	Make your favorite meal	Buy yourself something nice	Create a bucket list

DAY 21	DAY 22	DAY 23	DAY 24	DAY 25
Watch a movie or series	Write down your thoughts	Take a long shower or bath	Have a home spa day	Read inspirational quotes

DAY 26	DAY 27	DAY 28	DAY 29	DAY 30
Create a vision board	Spend some time outside	Do a hair mask	Write it all down in a journal	Take a power nap

NEW MONTH

BRAIN DUMP

....

....

....

....

....

....

....

....

....

....

....

....

....

Philippians 4:13

I can do all things through Christ who strengthens me.

MONTHLY PLANNER

Month _____

M	T	W	T	F	S	S

Psalm 139:14

I praise you because I am fearfully and wonderfully
made;
your works are wonderful,
I know that full well.

24

Monthly Budget

Income		
Income-1		
Income-2		
Other Income		
	Total Income	

Expenses	
Month	
Budget	

Bill To Be Paid	Due Date	Amount	Paid	Notes
	Total			

Monthly Summary		
Total Income	Total Expenses	Difference

Notes

25

Savings Goal

GOAL:		DATE	AMOUNT
SAVINGS:			
DEADLINE:			

TOTAL:

Weekly Planner

To Do List

This Week's Goal:

Important Tasks

Appointments

Proverbs 16:9
The heart of man plans his way, but the Lord
establishes his steps.

Weekly Goals

Day	Goals	Action Steps
Mon		
Tue		
Wed		
Thu		
Fri		
Sat		

GRATITUDE REMINDER

- **I am thankful for**

  _____
  _____
  _____

- **I am grateful for**

  _____
  _____
  _____

- **Notes**

Psalm 100:4-5
Enter his gates with thanksgiving
and his courts with praise;
give thanks to him and praise his
name.
For the Lord is good and his love
endures forever;
his faithfulness continues through all
generations.

MY WEEKLY PRAYER

_____

_____

_____

_____

_____

_____

_____

_____

_____

_____

_____

_____

_____

SCRIPTURE OF THE WEEK

PRAYER REQUEST

_____

_____

_____

_____

_____

_____

_____

_____

_____

_____

_____

_____

Week of: _____

Weekly Planner

To Do List

This Week's Goal:

Important Tasks

Appointments

Proverbs 16:9
The heart of man plans his way, but the Lord
establishes his steps.

Weekly Goals

Day	Goals	Action Steps
Mon		
Tue		
Wed		
Thu		
Fri		
Sat		

GRATITUDE REMINDER

- I am thankful for

- I am grateful for

- Notes

Psalm 100:4-5
Enter his gates with thanksgiving
and his courts with praise;
give thanks to him and praise his
name.
For the Lord is good and his love
endures forever;
his faithfulness continues through all
generations.

33

MY WEEKLY PRAYER

SCRIPTURE OF THE WEEK

PRAYER REQUEST

Week of: _____

Weekly Planner

This Week's Goal:

Important Tasks

Appointments

To Do List

Proverbs 16:9
The heart of man plans his way, but the Lord
establishes his steps.

Weekly Goals

Day	Goals	Action Steps
Mon		
Tue		
Wed		
Thu		
Fri		
Sat		

GRATITUDE REMINDER

- I am thankful for

- I am grateful for

- Notes

Psalm 100:4-5
Enter his gates with thanksgiving
and his courts with praise;
give thanks to him and praise his
name.
For the Lord is good and his love
endures forever;
his faithfulness continues through all
generations.

MY WEEKLY PRAYER

_____
_____
_____
_____
_____
_____
_____
_____
_____
_____
_____
_____
_____
_____
_____
_____

SCRIPTURE OF THE WEEK

PRAYER REQUEST

Week of: _____

Weekly Planner

To Do List

This Week's Goal:

Important Tasks

Appointments

Proverbs 16:9
The heart of man plans his way, but the Lord
establishes his steps.

39

Weekly Goals

Day	Goals	Action Steps
Mon		
Tue		
Wed		
Thu		
Fri		
Sat		

GRATITUDE REMINDER

- **I am thankful for**

- **I am grateful for**

- **Notes**

Psalm 100:4-5
Enter his gates with thanksgiving
and his courts with praise;
give thanks to him and praise his
name.
For the Lord is good and his love
endures forever;
his faithfulness continues through all
generations.

MY WEEKLY PRAYER

_____
_____
_____
_____
_____
_____
_____
_____
_____
_____
_____
_____
_____

SCRIPTURE OF THE WEEK

PRAYER REQUEST

_____
_____
_____
_____
_____
_____
_____
_____
_____
_____
_____
_____

Personal Reflection

Month:

BAD HABITS I NEED TO STOP

THINGS I REGRETTED NOT DOING

THINGS I LEARNED THIS MONTH

HOW TO BE A BETTER VERSION OF ME

Creativity
30 Day Challenge

Tidy your workspace	Take a different route	Read a nonfiction book	Start a dream journal	Go to bed earlier
Watch film	Try a new cuisine	Listen to classical music	Plan a holiday	Practice yoga
Try a DIY Project	Watch the sunrise	No phone day	Self care day	Try a DIY Project
Stretch	Read a book	Explore a new city	Go outside your comfort zone	Make moodboard
Go to bed earlier	Start a new hobby	Make time for exercise	Read a newspaper	Watch the sunset
Visit a museum	Learn a new skill	Create your ideal future	Do nothing	Go outside

NEW MONTH

BRAIN DUMP

....

....

....

....

....

....

....

....

....

....

....

....

Philippians 4:13

I can do all things through Christ who strengthens me.

MONTHLY PLANNER

Month _____

M	T	W	T	F	S	S

Psalm 139:14

I praise you because I am fearfully and wonderfully made;
your works are wonderful,
I know that full well.

Monthly Budget

Income			Expenses	
Income-1			Month	
Income-2				
Other Income			Budget	
	Total Income			

Bill To Be Paid	Due Date	Amount	Paid	Notes
	Total			

Monthly Summary		
Total Income	Total Expenses	Difference

Notes

Savings Goal

GOAL:

SAVINGS:

DEADLINE:

DATE	AMOUNT

TOTAL:

Week of: _____

Weekly Planner

This Week's Goal:

Important Tasks

Appointments

To Do List

Proverbs 16:9
The heart of man plans his way, but the Lord establishes his steps.

Weekly Goals

Day	Goals	Action Steps
Mon		
Tue		
Wed		
Thu		
Fri		
Sat		

GRATITUDE REMINDER

- I am thankful for

- I am grateful for

- Notes

Psalm 100:4-5
Enter his gates with thanksgiving
and his courts with praise;
give thanks to him and praise his
name.
For the Lord is good and his love
endures forever;
his faithfulness continues through all
generations.

MY WEEKLY PRAYER

_____
_____
_____
_____
_____
_____
_____
_____
_____
_____
_____

SCRIPTURE OF THE WEEK

PRAYER REQUEST

_____
_____
_____
_____
_____
_____
_____
_____
_____
_____
_____

Weekly Planner

To Do List

This Week's Goal:

Important Tasks

Appointments

Proverbs 16:9
The heart of man plans his way, but the Lord
establishes his steps.

Weekly Goals

Day	Goals	Action Steps
Mon		
Tue		
Wed		
Thu		
Fri		
Sat		

GRATITUDE REMINDER

- **I am thankful for**

- **I am grateful for**

- **Notes**

Psalm 100:4-5
Enter his gates with thanksgiving
and his courts with praise;
give thanks to him and praise his
name.
For the Lord is good and his love
endures forever;
his faithfulness continues through all
generations.

MY WEEKLY PRAYER

SCRIPTURE OF THE WEEK

PRAYER REQUEST

Weekly Planner

To Do List

This Week's Goal:

Important Tasks

Appointments

Proverbs 16:9
The heart of man plans his way, but the Lord
establishes his steps.

Weekly Goals

Day	Goals	Action Steps
Mon		
Tue		
Wed		
Thu		
Fri		
Sat		

GRATITUDE REMINDER

- **I am thankful for**

- **I am grateful for**

- **Notes**

Psalm 100:4-5
Enter his gates with thanksgiving
and his courts with praise;
give thanks to him and praise his
name.
For the Lord is good and his love
endures forever;
his faithfulness continues through all
generations.

MY WEEKLY PRAYER

_____
_____
_____
_____
_____
_____
_____
_____
_____
_____
_____
_____
_____
_____

SCRIPTURE OF THE WEEK

PRAYER REQUEST

_____
_____
_____
_____
_____
_____
_____
_____
_____
_____
_____
_____

Week of: _____

Weekly Planner

To Do List

This Week's Goal:

Important Tasks

Appointments

Proverbs 16:9
The heart of man plans his way, but the Lord establishes his steps.

61

Weekly Goals

Day	Goals	Action Steps
Mon		
Tue		
Wed		
Thu		
Fri		
Sat		

GRATITUDE REMINDER

- I am thankful for

- I am grateful for

- Notes

Psalm 100:4-5
Enter his gates with thanksgiving
and his courts with praise;
give thanks to him and praise his
name.
For the Lord is good and his love
endures forever;
his faithfulness continues through all
generations.

63

MY WEEKLY PRAYER

SCRIPTURE OF THE WEEK

PRAYER REQUEST

Personal Reflection

Month:

BAD HABITS I NEED TO STOP

THINGS I REGRETTED NOT DOING

THINGS I LEARNED THIS MONTH

HOW TO BE A BETTER VERSION OF ME

30 Day
Self-Care Challenge

◯ Stretch all your muscles	◯ Drink more water	◯ Go for a walk in nature	◯ Eat your favorite treat	◯ Go to bed early
◯ Listen to favorite song	◯ Eat vegetarian meals	◯ Take a nice bubble bath	◯ Cook your favorite meal	◯ Practice yoga
◯ Go on a solo date	◯ Journaling	◯ Give yourself a facial	◯ Practice gratitude	◯ Try a DIY Project
◯ Watch the sunrise	◯ Read a book	◯ Explore a new city	◯ Watch your favorite movie	◯ Give yourself a manicure
◯ Get some sunlight	◯ Start a new hobby	◯ Write out your goals	◯ Organize your closet	◯ Watch the sunset
◯ Give yourself a break	◯ Learn a new skill	◯ Create your ideal future	◯ Surround yourself with positivity	◯ Drink plenty of water

NEW MONTH

BRAIN DUMP

....

....

....

....

....

Philippians 4:13

....

I can do all things through Christ who strengthens me.

....

....

....

....

....

....

MONTHLY PLANNER

Month _____

M	T	W	T	F	S	S

Psalm 139:14

I praise you because I am fearfully and wonderfully made;
your works are wonderful,
I know that full well.

Monthly Budget

Income		
Income-1		
Income-2		
Other Income		
	Total Income	

Expenses	
Month	
Budget	

Bill To Be Paid	Due Date	Amount	Paid	Notes
	Total			

Monthly Summary		
Total Income	Total Expenses	Difference

Notes

69

Savings Goal

GOAL:

SAVINGS:

DEADLINE:

DATE	AMOUNT

TOTAL:

Week of: _____

Weekly Planner

To Do List

This Week's Goal:

Important Tasks

Appointments

Proverbs 16:9
The heart of man plans his way, but the Lord
establishes his steps.

Weekly Goals

Day	Goals	Action Steps
Mon		
Tue		
Wed		
Thu		
Fri		
Sat		

GRATITUDE REMINDER

- I am thankful for

- I am grateful for

- Notes

Psalm 100:4-5
Enter his gates with thanksgiving
and his courts with praise;
give thanks to him and praise his
name.
For the Lord is good and his love
endures forever;
his faithfulness continues through all
generations.

73

MY WEEKLY PRAYER

SCRIPTURE OF THE
WEEK

PRAYER REQUEST

Week of: _____

Weekly Planner

This Week's Goal:

To Do List

Important Tasks

Appointments

Proverbs 16:9
The heart of man plans his way, but the Lord
establishes his steps.

Weekly Goals

Day	Goals	Action Steps
Mon		
Tue		
Wed		
Thu		
Fri		
Sat		

GRATITUDE REMINDER

- **I am thankful for**

  _____
  _____
  _____

- **I am grateful for**

  _____
  _____
  _____

- **Notes**

Psalm 100:4-5
Enter his gates with thanksgiving
and his courts with praise;
give thanks to him and praise his
name.
For the Lord is good and his love
endures forever;
his faithfulness continues through all
generations.

MY WEEKLY PRAYER

_____
_____
_____
_____
_____
_____
_____
_____
_____
_____
_____
_____
_____
_____

SCRIPTURE OF THE WEEK

PRAYER REQUEST

_____
_____
_____
_____
_____
_____
_____
_____
_____
_____
_____
_____
_____

Week of: _____

Weekly Planner

This Week's Goal:

Important Tasks

Appointments

To Do List

Proverbs 16:9
The heart of man plans his way, but the Lord establishes his steps.

79

Weekly Goals

Day	Goals	Action Steps
Mon		
Tue		
Wed		
Thu		
Fri		
Sat		

GRATITUDE REMINDER

- **I am thankful for**

  _____
  _____
  _____

- **I am grateful for**

  _____
  _____
  _____

- **Notes**

Psalm 100:4-5
Enter his gates with thanksgiving
and his courts with praise;
give thanks to him and praise his
name.
For the Lord is good and his love
endures forever;
his faithfulness continues through all
generations.

MY WEEKLY PRAYER

_____
_____
_____
_____
_____
_____
_____
_____
_____
_____
_____
_____
_____

SCRIPTURE OF THE WEEK

PRAYER REQUEST

_____
_____
_____
_____
_____
_____
_____
_____
_____
_____
_____

Week of: _____

Weekly Planner

This Week's Goal:

To Do List

Important Tasks

Appointments

Proverbs 16:9
The heart of man plans his way, but the Lord
establishes his steps.

Weekly Goals

Day	Goals	Action Steps
Mon		
Tue		
Wed		
Thu		
Fri		
Sat		

GRATITUDE REMINDER

- **I am thankful for**

- **I am grateful for**

- **Notes**

Psalm 100:4-5
Enter his gates with thanksgiving
and his courts with praise;
give thanks to him and praise his
name.
For the Lord is good and his love
endures forever;
his faithfulness continues through all
generations.

MY WEEKLY PRAYER

_____
_____
_____
_____
_____
_____
_____
_____
_____
_____
_____
_____
_____
_____
_____

SCRIPTURE OF THE WEEK

PRAYER REQUEST

Personal Reflection

Month:

BAD HABITS I NEED TO STOP

THINGS I REGRETTED NOT DOING

THINGS I LEARNED THIS MONTH

HOW TO BE A BETTER VERSION OF ME

30 Days of Gratitude

Day 1 ....

Day 2 ....

Day 3 ....

Day 4 ....

Day 5 ....

Day 6 ....

Day 7 ....

Day 8 ....

Day 9 ....

Day 10 ....

Day 11 ....

Day 12 ....

Day 13 ....

Day 14 ....

Day 15 ....

Day 16 ....

Day 17 ....

Day 18 ....

Day 19 ....

Day 20 ....

Day 21 ....

Day 22 ....

Day 23 ....

Day 24 ....

Day 25 ....

Day 26 ....

Day 27 ....

Day 28 ....

Day 29 ....

Day 30 ....

NEW MONTH

BRAIN DUMP

Philippians 4:13

I can do all things through Christ who strengthens me.

MONTHLY PLANNER

Month _____

M	T	W	T	F	S	S

Psalm 139:14

I praise you because I am fearfully and wonderfully made;
your works are wonderful,
I know that full well.

Monthly Budget

Income			Expenses	
Income-1			Month	
Income-2				
Other Income			Budget	
	Total Income			

Bill To Be Paid	Due Date	Amount	Paid	Notes
	Total			

Monthly Summary

Total Income	Total Expenses	Difference

Notes

_____
_____
_____
_____
_____

Savings Goal

GOAL:

SAVINGS:

DEADLINE:

DATE	AMOUNT

TOTAL:

Week of: _____

Weekly Planner

This Week's Goal:

To Do List

Important Tasks

Appointments

Proverbs 16:9
The heart of man plans his way, but the Lord
establishes his steps.

93

Weekly Goals

Day	Goals	Action Steps
Mon		
Tue		
Wed		
Thu		
Fri		
Sat		

GRATITUDE REMINDER

- I am thankful for

- I am grateful for

- Notes

Psalm 100:4-5
Enter his gates with thanksgiving
and his courts with praise;
give thanks to him and praise his
name.
For the Lord is good and his love
endures forever;
his faithfulness continues through all
generations.

MY WEEKLY PRAYER

_____
_____
_____
_____
_____
_____
_____
_____
_____
_____
_____
_____
_____

SCRIPTURE OF THE WEEK

PRAYER REQUEST

Week of: _____

Weekly Planner

This Week's Goal:

Important Tasks

Appointments

To Do List

Proverbs 16:9
The heart of man plans his way, but the Lord
establishes his steps.

Weekly Goals

Day	Goals	Action Steps
Mon		
Tue		
Wed		
Thu		
Fri		
Sat		

GRATITUDE REMINDER

- **I am thankful for**

- **I am grateful for**

- **Notes**

Psalm 100:4-5
Enter his gates with thanksgiving
and his courts with praise;
give thanks to him and praise his
name.
For the Lord is good and his love
endures forever;
his faithfulness continues through all
generations.

_____
_____
_____
_____
_____
_____
_____
_____
_____
_____
_____
_____
_____

SCRIPTURE OF THE WEEK

PRAYER REQUEST

_____
_____
_____
_____
_____
_____
_____
_____
_____
_____
_____
_____
_____

Week of: _____

Weekly Planner

This Week's Goal:

Important Tasks

Appointments

To Do List

Proverbs 16:9
The heart of man plans his way, but the Lord
establishes his steps.

Weekly Goals

Day	Goals	Action Steps
Mon		
Tue		
Wed		
Thu		
Fri		
Sat		

GRATITUDE REMINDER

- **I am thankful for**

- **I am grateful for**

- **Notes**

Psalm 100:4-5
Enter his gates with thanksgiving
and his courts with praise;
give thanks to him and praise his
name.
For the Lord is good and his love
endures forever;
his faithfulness continues through all
generations.

MY WEEKLY PRAYER

_____
_____
_____
_____
_____
_____
_____
_____
_____
_____
_____
_____
_____
_____
_____

SCRIPTURE OF THE WEEK

PRAYER REQUEST

_____
_____
_____
_____
_____
_____
_____
_____
_____
_____
_____
_____
_____
_____

Week of: _____

Weekly Planner

This Week's Goal:

Important Tasks

Appointments

To Do List

Proverbs 16:9
The heart of man plans his way, but the Lord
establishes his steps.

Weekly Goals

Day	Goals	Action Steps
Mon		
Tue		
Wed		
Thu		
Fri		
Sat		

GRATITUDE REMINDER

- I am thankful for

- I am grateful for

- Notes

Psalm 100:4-5
Enter his gates with thanksgiving
and his courts with praise;
give thanks to him and praise his
name.
For the Lord is good and his love
endures forever;
his faithfulness continues through all
generations.

MY WEEKLY PRAYER

SCRIPTURE OF THE WEEK

PRAYER REQUEST

Personal Reflection

Month:

BAD HABITS I NEED TO STOP

THINGS I REGRETTED NOT DOING

THINGS I LEARNED THIS MONTH

HOW TO BE A BETTER VERSION OF ME

Self Love Challenge

Forgive yourself	Practice Self-care	Do a DIY Project	Make a playlist
Put on your favorite outfit	Go for a 30-minute walk	Read a self-help book	Buy a bucket of flower
Let the sunshine in	Write down a journal	Make yourself a priority	Start a Gratitude journal
Make your dreams come true	Learn something new	Pamper yourself	Sleep for 8 hours
Create a bucket list	Practice yoga	Take a walk in the nature	Write down your goals
Practice a hobby	Spend time with a friend	Compliment yourself	Practice saying no

NEW MONTH

BRAIN DUMP

Philippians
4:13

I can do all
things
through
Christ who
strengthens
me.

MONTHLY PLANNER

Month _____

M	T	W	T	F	S	S

Psalm 139:14

I praise you because I am fearfully and wonderfully made;
your works are wonderful,
I know that full well.

Philippians 4:19
And my God will meet all your needs according to the riches of his glory in Christ Jesus.

Monthly Budget

Income		
Income-1		
Income-2		
Other Income		
	Total Income	

Expenses	
Month	
Budget	

Bill To Be Paid	Due Date	Amount	Paid	Notes
	Total			

Monthly Summary		
Total Income	Total Expenses	Difference

Notes

Savings Goal

GOAL:

SAVINGS:

DEADLINE:

DATE	AMOUNT

TOTAL:

Week of: _____

Weekly Planner

To Do List

This Week's Goal:

Important Tasks

Appointments

- [ ]
- [ ]
- [ ]
- [ ]
- [ ]
- [ ]
- [ ]

Proverbs 16:9
The heart of man plans his way, but the Lord establishes his steps.

Weekly Goals

Day	Goals	Action Steps
Mon		
Tue		
Wed		
Thu		
Fri		
Sat		

GRATITUDE REMINDER

- **I am thankful for**

  _____

  _____

  _____

- **I am grateful for**

  _____

  _____

  _____

- **Notes**

Psalm 100:4-5
Enter his gates with thanksgiving
and his courts with praise;
give thanks to him and praise his
name.
For the Lord is good and his love
endures forever;
his faithfulness continues through all
generations.

MY WEEKLY PRAYER

_____
_____
_____
_____
_____
_____
_____
_____
_____
_____
_____
_____
_____
_____

SCRIPTURE OF THE WEEK

PRAYER REQUEST

_____
_____
_____
_____
_____
_____
_____
_____
_____
_____
_____
_____

Week of: _____

Weekly Planner

This Week's Goal:

Important Tasks

Appointments

To Do List

Proverbs 16:9
The heart of man plans his way, but the Lord establishes his steps.

Weekly Goals

Day	Goals	Action Steps
Mon		
Tue		
Wed		
Thu		
Fri		
Sat		

GRATITUDE REMINDER

- **I am thankful for**

  _____
  _____
  _____

- **I am grateful for**

  _____
  _____
  _____

- **Notes**

Psalm 100:4-5
Enter his gates with thanksgiving
and his courts with praise;
give thanks to him and praise his
name.
For the Lord is good and his love
endures forever;
his faithfulness continues through all
generations.

MY WEEKLY PRAYER

_____
_____
_____
_____
_____
_____
_____
_____
_____
_____
_____
_____
_____

SCRIPTURE OF THE WEEK

PRAYER REQUEST

_____
_____
_____
_____
_____
_____
_____
_____
_____
_____
_____
_____

Week of: _____

Weekly Planner

This Week's Goal:

To Do List

Important Tasks

Appointments

Proverbs 16:9
The heart of man plans his way, but the Lord
establishes his steps.

Weekly Goals

Day	Goals	Action Steps
Mon		
Tue		
Wed		
Thu		
Fri		
Sat		

GRATITUDE REMINDER

- I am thankful for

- I am grateful for

- Notes

Psalm 100:4-5
Enter his gates with thanksgiving
and his courts with praise;
give thanks to him and praise his
name.
For the Lord is good and his love
endures forever;
his faithfulness continues through all
generations.

MY WEEKLY PRAYER

_____
_____
_____
_____
_____
_____
_____
_____
_____
_____
_____
_____

SCRIPTURE OF THE WEEK

PRAYER REQUEST

_____
_____
_____
_____
_____
_____
_____
_____
_____
_____
_____
_____

Weekly Planner

This Week's Goal:

Important Tasks

Appointments

To Do List

Proverbs 16:9
The heart of man plans his way, but the Lord
establishes his steps.

Weekly Goals

Day	Goals	Action Steps
Mon		
Tue		
Wed		
Thu		
Fri		
Sat		

GRATITUDE REMINDER

- **I am thankful for**

- **I am grateful for**

- **Notes**

Psalm 100:4-5
Enter his gates with thanksgiving
and his courts with praise;
give thanks to him and praise his
name.
For the Lord is good and his love
endures forever;
his faithfulness continues through all
generations.

MY WEEKLY PRAYER

SCRIPTURE OF THE WEEK

PRAYER REQUEST

Personal Reflection

Month:

BAD HABITS I NEED TO STOP

THINGS I REGRETTED NOT DOING

THINGS I LEARNED THIS MONTH

HOW TO BE A BETTER VERSION OF ME

131

12 Days
Meditation

Challenge

1 Focus On Your Breath	**2** Think Of Someone You Love	**3** List Things You Are Grateful For	**4** Says Positive Things About Yourself
5 List Things You Are Grateful For	**6** List Amazing Things That Happened Today	**7** Visualize A Place You Love	**8** Take Few Breath Outside
9 Say Compliments To Yourself	**10** List Things You Are Grateful For	**11** List 5 Persons You Love	**12** Focus On Your Breath

Do not be conformed to this world, but be transformed by the renewal of your mind, that by testing you may discern what is the will of God, what is good and acceptable and perfect.

Romans 12:2

NEW MONTH

BRAIN DUMP

....
....
....
....
....
....
....
....
....
....
....
....
....
....

Philippians 4:13

I can do all things through Christ who strengthens me.

MONTHLY PLANNER

Month _____

M	T	W	T	F	S	S

Psalm 139:14

I praise you because I am fearfully and wonderfully made;
your works are wonderful,
I know that full well.

Monthly Budget

Income			Expenses	
Income-1			Month	
Income-2				
Other Income			Budget	
	Total Income			

Bill To Be Paid	Due Date	Amount	Paid	Notes
	Total			

Monthly Summary

Total Income	Total Expenses	Difference

Notes

Savings Goal

GOAL:		DATE	AMOUNT
SAVINGS:			
DEADLINE:			

TOTAL:

Week of: _____

Weekly Planner

This Week's Goal:

Important Tasks

Appointments

To Do List

Proverbs 16:9
The heart of man plans his way, but the Lord
establishes his steps.

Weekly Goals

Day	Goals	Action Steps
Mon		
Tue		
Wed		
Thu		
Fri		
Sat		

GRATITUDE REMINDER

- **I am thankful for**

- **I am grateful for**

- **Notes**

Psalm 100:4-5
Enter his gates with thanksgiving
and his courts with praise;
give thanks to him and praise his
name.
For the Lord is good and his love
endures forever;
his faithfulness continues through all
generations.

MY WEEKLY PRAYER

SCRIPTURE OF THE WEEK

PRAYER REQUEST

Week of: _____

Weekly Planner

This Week's Goal:

Important Tasks

Appointments

To Do List

Proverbs 16:9
The heart of man plans his way, but the Lord
establishes his steps.

Weekly Goals

Day	Goals	Action Steps
Mon		
Tue		
Wed		
Thu		
Fri		
Sat		

GRATITUDE REMINDER

- **I am thankful for**

- **I am grateful for**

- **Notes**

Psalm 100:4-5
Enter his gates with thanksgiving
and his courts with praise;
give thanks to him and praise his
name.
For the Lord is good and his love
endures forever;
his faithfulness continues through all
generations.

MY WEEKLY PRAYER

SCRIPTURE OF THE WEEK

PRAYER REQUEST

Week of: _____

Weekly Planner

This Week's Goal:

Important Tasks

Appointments

To Do List

Proverbs 16:9
The heart of man plans his way, but the Lord establishes his steps.

145

Weekly Goals

Day	Goals	Action Steps
Mon		
Tue		
Wed		
Thu		
Fri		
Sat		

GRATITUDE REMINDER

- I am thankful for

- I am grateful for

- Notes

Psalm 100:4-5
Enter his gates with thanksgiving
and his courts with praise;
give thanks to him and praise his
name.
For the Lord is good and his love
endures forever;
his faithfulness continues through all
generations.

147

MY WEEKLY PRAYER

SCRIPTURE OF THE WEEK

PRAYER REQUEST

Weekly Planner

This Week's Goal:

Important Tasks

Appointments

To Do List

Proverbs 16:9
The heart of man plans his way, but the Lord
establishes his steps.

149

Weekly Goals

Day	Goals	Action Steps
Mon		
Tue		
Wed		
Thu		
Fri		
Sat		

GRATITUDE REMINDER

- ## I am thankful for

- ## I am grateful for

- ## Notes

Psalm 100:4-5
Enter his gates with thanksgiving
and his courts with praise;
give thanks to him and praise his
name.
For the Lord is good and his love
endures forever;
his faithfulness continues through all
generations.

MY WEEKLY PRAYER

_____
_____
_____
_____
_____
_____
_____
_____
_____
_____
_____
_____
_____
_____
_____

SCRIPTURE OF THE WEEK

PRAYER REQUEST

_____
_____
_____
_____
_____
_____
_____
_____
_____
_____
_____
_____
_____
_____

Personal Reflection

Month:

BAD HABITS I NEED TO STOP

THINGS I REGRETTED NOT DOING

THINGS I LEARNED THIS MONTH

HOW TO BE A BETTER VERSION OF ME

30 DAY BEACH BODY CHALLENGE

1	2	3	4	5
50 crunches 2x 60 second plank	50 crunches 2x 60 second plank	50 crunches 2x 60 second plank	50 crunches 2x 60 second plank	50 crunches 2x 60 second plank
6	7	8	9	10
50 crunches 2x 60 second plank	50 crunches 2x 60 second plank	50 crunches 2x 60 second plank	50 crunches 2x 60 second plank	50 crunches 2x 60 second plank
11	12	13	14	15
50 crunches 2x 60 second plank	50 crunches 2x 60 second plank	50 crunches 2x 60 second plank	50 crunches 2x 60 second plank	50 crunches 2x 60 second plank
16	17	18	19	20
50 crunches 2x 60 second plank	50 crunches 2x 60 second plank	50 crunches 2x 60 second plank	50 crunches 2x 60 second plank	50 crunches 2x 60 second plank
21	22	23	24	25
50 crunches 2x 60 second plank	50 crunches 2x 60 second plank	50 crunches 2x 60 second plank	50 crunches 2x 60 second plank	50 crunches 2x 60 second plank
26	27	28	29	30
50 crunches 2x 60 second plank	50 crunches 2x 60 second plank	50 crunches 2x 60 second plank	50 crunches 2x 60 second plank	50 crunches 2x 60 second plank

NEW MONTH

BRAIN DUMP

Philippians 4:13

I can do all things through Christ who strengthens me.

MONTHLY PLANNER

Month _____

M	T	W	T	F	S	S

Psalm 139:14

I praise you because I am fearfully and wonderfully made;
your works are wonderful,
I know that full well.

Philippians 4:19
And my God will meet all your needs according to the riches of his glory in Christ Jesus.

Monthly Budget

Income			Expenses	
Income-1			Month	
Income-2				
Other Income			Budget	
	Total Income			

Bill To Be Paid	Due Date	Amount	Paid	Notes
	Total			

Monthly Summary		
Total Income	Total Expenses	Difference

Notes

157

Savings Goal

GOAL:

SAVINGS:

DEADLINE:

DATE	AMOUNT

TOTAL:

Week of: _____

Weekly Planner

This Week's Goal:

Important Tasks

Appointments

To Do List

Proverbs 16:9
The heart of man plans his way, but the Lord
establishes his steps.

Weekly Goals

Day	Goals	Action Steps
Mon		
Tue		
Wed		
Thu		
Fri		
Sat		

GRATITUDE REMINDER

- **I am thankful for**

- **I am grateful for**

- **Notes**

Psalm 100:4-5
Enter his gates with thanksgiving
and his courts with praise;
give thanks to him and praise his
name.
For the Lord is good and his love
endures forever;
his faithfulness continues through all
generations.

MY WEEKLY PRAYER

_____
_____
_____
_____
_____
_____
_____
_____
_____
_____
_____
_____
_____
_____
_____

SCRIPTURE OF THE WEEK

PRAYER REQUEST

_____
_____
_____
_____
_____
_____
_____
_____
_____
_____
_____
_____
_____
_____
_____

Week of: _____

Weekly Planner

This Week's Goal:

Important Tasks

Appointments

To Do List

Proverbs 16:9
The heart of man plans his way, but the Lord
establishes his steps.

163

Weekly Goals

Day	Goals	Action Steps
Mon		
Tue		
Wed		
Thu		
Fri		
Sat		

GRATITUDE REMINDER

- **I am thankful for**

- **I am grateful for**

- **Notes**

Psalm 100:4-5
Enter his gates with thanksgiving
and his courts with praise;
give thanks to him and praise his name.
For the Lord is good and his love
endures forever;
his faithfulness continues through all
generations.

MY WEEKLY PRAYER

_____
_____
_____
_____
_____
_____
_____
_____
_____
_____
_____
_____
_____

SCRIPTURE OF THE WEEK

PRAYER REQUEST

_____
_____
_____
_____
_____
_____
_____
_____
_____
_____
_____
_____
_____
_____

Weekly Planner

To Do List

This Week's Goal:

Important Tasks

Appointments

Proverbs 16:9
The heart of man plans his way, but the Lord
establishes his steps.

Weekly Goals

Day	Goals	Action Steps
Mon		
Tue		
Wed		
Thu		
Fri		
Sat		

GRATITUDE REMINDER

- **I am thankful for**

- **I am grateful for**

- **Notes**

Psalm 100:4-5
Enter his gates with thanksgiving
and his courts with praise;
give thanks to him and praise his
name.
For the Lord is good and his love
endures forever;
his faithfulness continues through all
generations.

MY WEEKLY PRAYER

SCRIPTURE OF THE WEEK

PRAYER REQUEST

Week of: _____

Weekly Planner

This Week's Goal:

Important Tasks

Appointments

To Do List

Proverbs 16:9
The heart of man plans his way, but the Lord establishes his steps.

Weekly Goals

Day	Goals	Action Steps
Mon		
Tue		
Wed		
Thu		
Fri		
Sat		

GRATITUDE REMINDER

- **I am thankful for**

- **I am grateful for**

- **Notes**

Psalm 100:4-5
Enter his gates with thanksgiving
and his courts with praise;
give thanks to him and praise his
name.
For the Lord is good and his love
endures forever;
his faithfulness continues through all
generations.

MY WEEKLY PRAYER

SCRIPTURE OF THE WEEK

PRAYER REQUEST

Personal Reflection

Month:

BAD HABITS I NEED TO STOP

THINGS I REGRETTED NOT DOING

THINGS I LEARNED THIS MONTH

HOW TO BE A BETTER VERSION OF ME

BOOK _____

30 DAY
Reading Challenge
Date / Chapter / Pages

- [ ]
- [ ]
- [ ]
- [ ]
- [ ]
- [ ]
- [ ]
- [ ]
- [ ]
- [ ]
- [ ]
- [ ]

COMPLETE ONE BOOK

NEW MONTH

BRAIN DUMP

....

....

....

....

....

....

....

....

....

....

....

....

....

Philippians 4:13

I can do all things through Christ who strengthens me.

MONTHLY PLANNER

Month _____

M	T	W	T	F	S	S

Psalm 139:14

I praise you because I am fearfully and wonderfully
made;
your works are wonderful,
I know that full well.

Monthly Budget

Income		
Income-1		
Income-2		
Other Income		
	Total Income	

Expenses	
Month	
Budget	

Bill To Be Paid	Due Date	Amount	Paid	Notes
	Total			

Monthly Summary

Total Income	Total Expenses	Difference

Notes

Savings Goal

GOAL:

SAVINGS:

DEADLINE:

DATE	AMOUNT

TOTAL:

Week of: _____

Weekly Planner

This Week's Goal:

To Do List

Important Tasks

Appointments

Proverbs 16:9
The heart of man plans his way, but the Lord establishes his steps.

Weekly Goals

Day	Goals	Action Steps
Mon		
Tue		
Wed		
Thu		
Fri		
Sat		

GRATITUDE REMINDER

- **I am thankful for**

- **I am grateful for**

- **Notes**

Psalm 100:4-5
Enter his gates with thanksgiving
and his courts with praise;
give thanks to him and praise his
name.
For the Lord is good and his love
endures forever;
his faithfulness continues through all
generations.

MY WEEKLY PRAYER

SCRIPTURE OF THE WEEK

PRAYER REQUEST

Week of: _____

Weekly Planner

This Week's Goal:

Important Tasks

Appointments

To Do List

Proverbs 16:9
The heart of man plans his way, but the Lord
establishes his steps.

Weekly Goals

Day	Goals	Action Steps
Mon		
Tue		
Wed		
Thu		
Fri		
Sat		

GRATITUDE REMINDER

- I am thankful for

- I am grateful for

- Notes

Psalm 100:4-5
Enter his gates with thanksgiving
and his courts with praise;
give thanks to him and praise his
name.
For the Lord is good and his love
endures forever;
his faithfulness continues through all
generations.

MY WEEKLY PRAYER

SCRIPTURE OF THE WEEK

PRAYER REQUEST

Week of: _____

Weekly Planner

This Week's Goal:

To Do List

Important Tasks

Appointments

Proverbs 16:9
The heart of man plans his way, but the Lord
establishes his steps.

Weekly Goals

Day	Goals	Action Steps
Mon		
Tue		
Wed		
Thu		
Fri		
Sat		

GRATITUDE REMINDER

- **I am thankful for**

- **I am grateful for**

- **Notes**

Psalm 100:4-5
Enter his gates with thanksgiving
and his courts with praise;
give thanks to him and praise his
name.
For the Lord is good and his love
endures forever;
his faithfulness continues through all
generations.

MY WEEKLY PRAYER

_____
_____
_____
_____
_____
_____
_____
_____
_____
_____
_____
_____

SCRIPTURE OF THE WEEK

PRAYER REQUEST

_____
_____
_____
_____
_____
_____
_____
_____
_____
_____
_____
_____
_____

Week of: _____

Weekly Planner

This Week's Goal:

Important Tasks

Appointments

To Do List

Proverbs 16:9
The heart of man plans his way, but the Lord
establishes his steps.

Weekly Goals

Day	Goals	Action Steps
Mon		
Tue		
Wed		
Thu		
Fri		
Sat		

GRATITUDE REMINDER

- **I am thankful for**

- **I am grateful for**

- **Notes**

Psalm 100:4-5
Enter his gates with thanksgiving
and his courts with praise;
give thanks to him and praise his
name.
For the Lord is good and his love
endures forever;
his faithfulness continues through all
generations.

MY WEEKLY PRAYER

SCRIPTURE OF THE WEEK

PRAYER REQUEST

Personal Reflection

Month:

BAD HABITS I NEED TO STOP

THINGS I REGRETTED NOT DOING

THINGS I LEARNED THIS MONTH

HOW TO BE A BETTER VERSION OF ME

Self Care Challenge

Write down your goal	Drink enough water	Eat healthy food	Go for a long walk
Spend time alone	Sleep for 8 hours	Meditate for 5 minutes	Create a new playlist
Cook your favorite meal	Try a new exercise	No TV night	Take a cold shower
Walk in the nature	Start journaling	Do a quick workout	Create a mood board

Focus on the steps
in front of you,
not the whole staircase.

NEW MONTH

BRAIN DUMP

....

....

....

....

....

....

....

....

....

....

....

....

....

....

Philippians
4:13

I can do all
things
through
Christ who
strengthens
me.

MONTHLY PLANNER

Month _____

M	T	W	T	F	S	S

Psalm 139:14

I praise you because I am fearfully and wonderfully made;
your works are wonderful,
I know that full well.

And my God will meet all your needs according to the riches of his glory in Christ Jesus.

Monthly Budget

Income			Expenses	
Income-1			Month	
Income-2				
Other Income			Budget	
	Total Income			

Bill To Be Paid	Due Date	Amount	Paid	Notes
	Total			

Monthly Summary

Total Income	Total Expenses	Difference

Notes

Savings Goal

GOAL:

SAVINGS:

DEADLINE:

DATE	AMOUNT

TOTAL:

Week of: _____

Weekly Planner

This Week's Goal:

Important Tasks

Appointments

To Do List

Proverbs 16:9
The heart of man plans his way, but the Lord
establishes his steps.

Weekly Goals

Day	Goals	Action Steps
Mon		
Tue		
Wed		
Thu		
Fri		
Sat		

GRATITUDE REMINDER

- **I am thankful for**

- **I am grateful for**

- **Notes**

Psalm 100:4-5
Enter his gates with thanksgiving
and his courts with praise;
give thanks to him and praise his
name.
For the Lord is good and his love
endures forever;
his faithfulness continues through all
generations.

MY WEEKLY PRAYER

SCRIPTURE OF THE WEEK

PRAYER REQUEST

Week of: _____

Weekly Planner

This Week's Goal:

Important Tasks

Appointments

To Do List

Proverbs 16:9
The heart of man plans his way, but the Lord
establishes his steps.

Weekly Goals

Day	Goals	Action Steps
Mon		
Tue		
Wed		
Thu		
Fri		
Sat		

GRATITUDE REMINDER

- ## I am thankful for

- ## I am grateful for

- ## Notes

Psalm 100:4-5
Enter his gates with thanksgiving
and his courts with praise;
give thanks to him and praise his
name.
For the Lord is good and his love
endures forever;
his faithfulness continues through all
generations.

MY WEEKLY PRAYER

_____
_____
_____
_____
_____
_____
_____
_____
_____
_____
_____
_____
_____
_____
_____
_____

SCRIPTURE OF THE WEEK

PRAYER REQUEST

_____
_____
_____
_____
_____
_____
_____
_____
_____
_____
_____
_____
_____
_____

Week of: _____

Weekly Planner

This Week's Goal:

Important Tasks

Appointments

To Do List

Proverbs 16:9
The heart of man plans his way, but the Lord
establishes his steps.

211

Weekly Goals

Day	Goals	Action Steps
Mon		
Tue		
Wed		
Thu		
Fri		
Sat		

GRATITUDE REMINDER

- **I am thankful for**

- **I am grateful for**

- **Notes**

Psalm 100:4-5
Enter his gates with thanksgiving
and his courts with praise;
give thanks to him and praise his
name.
For the Lord is good and his love
endures forever;
his faithfulness continues through all
generations.

MY WEEKLY PRAYER

_____

SCRIPTURE OF THE WEEK

PRAYER REQUEST

Week of: _____

Weekly Planner

This Week's Goal:

To Do List

Important Tasks

Appointments

Proverbs 16:9
The heart of man plans his way, but the Lord
establishes his steps.

Weekly Goals

Day	Goals	Action Steps
Mon		
Tue		
Wed		
Thu		
Fri		
Sat		

GRATITUDE REMINDER

- **I am thankful for**

- **I am grateful for**

- **Notes**

Psalm 100:4-5
Enter his gates with thanksgiving
and his courts with praise;
give thanks to him and praise his
name.
For the Lord is good and his love
endures forever;
his faithfulness continues through all
generations.

MY WEEKLY PRAYER

SCRIPTURE OF THE WEEK

PRAYER REQUEST

Personal Reflection

Month:

BAD HABITS I NEED TO STOP

THINGS I REGRETTED NOT DOING

THINGS I LEARNED THIS MONTH

HOW TO BE A BETTER VERSION OF ME

Create A Morning Routine

Ex:

Wake Up

Brush Teeth & Wash Face

Prayer & Devotion

Exercise

Eat a Healthy Breakfast

Morning Journal Pages

Read For 20 Minutes

NEW MONTH

BRAIN DUMP

....

....

....

....

....

....

....

....

....

....

....

....

....

Philippians 4:13

I can do all things through Christ who strengthens me.

MONTHLY PLANNER

Month _____

M	T	W	T	F	S	S

Psalm 139:14

I praise you because I am fearfully and wonderfully made;
your works are wonderful,
I know that full well.

Monthly Budget

Income			Expenses	
Income-1			Month	
Income-2				
Other Income			Budget	
	Total Income			

Bill To Be Paid	Due Date	Amount	Paid	Notes
	Total			

Monthly Summary

Total Income	Total Expenses	Difference

Notes

_____
_____
_____
_____
_____

Savings Goal

GOAL:

SAVINGS:

DEADLINE:

DATE	AMOUNT

TOTAL:

Week of: _____

Weekly Planner

This Week's Goal:

Important Tasks

Appointments

To Do List

Proverbs 16:9
The heart of man plans his way, but the Lord establishes his steps.

Weekly Goals

Day	Goals	Action Steps
Mon		
Tue		
Wed		
Thu		
Fri		
Sat		

GRATITUDE REMINDER

- **I am thankful for**

  _____
  _____
  _____

- **I am grateful for**

  _____
  _____
  _____

- **Notes**

Psalm 100:4-5
Enter his gates with thanksgiving
and his courts with praise;
give thanks to him and praise his
name.
For the Lord is good and his love
endures forever;
his faithfulness continues through all
generations.

MY WEEKLY PRAYER

SCRIPTURE OF THE WEEK

PRAYER REQUEST

Week of: _____

Weekly Planner

This Week's Goal:

Important Tasks

Appointments

To Do List

Proverbs 16:9
The heart of man plans his way, but the Lord establishes his steps.

Weekly Goals

Day	Goals	Action Steps
Mon		
Tue		
Wed		
Thu		
Fri		
Sat		

GRATITUDE REMINDER

- **I am thankful for**

- **I am grateful for**

- **Notes**

Psalm 100:4-5
Enter his gates with thanksgiving
and his courts with praise;
give thanks to him and praise his
name.
For the Lord is good and his love
endures forever;
his faithfulness continues through all
generations.

MY WEEKLY PRAYER

_____
_____
_____
_____
_____
_____
_____
_____
_____
_____
_____
_____
_____

SCRIPTURE OF THE WEEK

PRAYER REQUEST

_____
_____
_____
_____
_____
_____
_____
_____
_____
_____
_____
_____

Week of: _____

Weekly Planner

This Week's Goal:

Important Tasks

Appointments

To Do List

Proverbs 16:9
The heart of man plans his way, but the Lord establishes his steps.

Weekly Goals

Day	Goals	Action Steps
Mon		
Tue		
Wed		
Thu		
Fri		
Sat		

GRATITUDE REMINDER

- **I am thankful for**

  _____

  _____

  _____

- **I am grateful for**

  _____

  _____

  _____

- **Notes**

Psalm 100:4-5
Enter his gates with thanksgiving
and his courts with praise;
give thanks to him and praise his
name.
For the Lord is good and his love
endures forever;
his faithfulness continues through all
generations.

MY WEEKLY PRAYER

SCRIPTURE OF THE WEEK

PRAYER REQUEST

Personal Reflection

Month:

BAD HABITS I NEED TO STOP

THINGS I REGRETTED NOT DOING

THINGS I LEARNED THIS MONTH

HOW TO BE A BETTER VERSION OF ME

Weekly Goals

Day	Goals	Action Steps
Mon		
Tue		
Wed		
Thu		
Fri		
Sat		

GRATITUDE REMINDER

- **I am thankful for**

- **I am grateful for**

- **Notes**

Psalm 100:4-5
Enter his gates with thanksgiving
and his courts with praise;
give thanks to him and praise his
name.
For the Lord is good and his love
endures forever;
his faithfulness continues through all
generations.

MY WEEKLY PRAYER

_____
_____
_____
_____
_____
_____
_____
_____
_____
_____
_____
_____
_____

SCRIPTURE OF THE WEEK

PRAYER REQUEST

_____
_____
_____
_____
_____
_____
_____
_____
_____
_____
_____
_____
_____
_____

Personal Reflection

Month: _____

BAD HABITS I NEED TO STOP

THINGS I REGRETTED NOT DOING

THINGS I LEARNED THIS MONTH

HOW TO BE A BETTER VERSION OF ME

7 DAY WORKOUT CHALLENGE

MONDAY

10 Push up
20 Squats
15 Lunges
40 Chrunches
30 Sec Plank

30 Jumping jacks
5 Min walk

TUESDAY

10 Push up
20 Squats
15 Lunges
30 Chrunches

WEDNESDAY

20 Push up
25 Squats
15 Lunges
50 Chrunches
30 Sec Plank

30 Jumping jacks
10 Min walk

THURSDAY

20 Push up
25 Squats
20 Lunges
35 Chrunches

FRIDAY

20 Push up
25 Squats
15 Lunges
50 Chrunches
30 Sec Plank

SATURDAY

20 Push up
25 Squats
20 Lunges
35 Chrunches

SUNDAY

Rest

NEW MONTH

BRAIN DUMP

....

....

....

....

....

....

....

....

....

....

....

....

Philippians 4:13

I can do all things through Christ who strengthens me.

MONTHLY PLANNER

Month _____

M	T	W	T	F	S	S

Psalm 139:14

I praise you because I am fearfully and wonderfully made;
your works are wonderful,
I know that full well.

244

Philippians 4:19
And my God will meet all your needs according to the riches of his glory in Christ Jesus.

Monthly Budget

Income		
Income-1		
Income-2		
Other Income		
	Total Income	

Expenses	
Month	
Budget	

Bill To Be Paid	Due Date	Amount	Paid	Notes
	Total			

Monthly Summary		
Total Income	Total Expenses	Difference

Notes

Savings Goal

GOAL:

SAVINGS:

DEADLINE:

DATE	AMOUNT

TOTAL:

Weekly Planner

This Week's Goal:

Important Tasks

Appointments

To Do List

Proverbs 16:9
The heart of man plans his way, but the Lord
establishes his steps.

Weekly Goals

Day	Goals	Action Steps
Mon		
Tue		
Wed		
Thu		
Fri		
Sat		

GRATITUDE REMINDER

- **I am thankful for**

- **I am grateful for**

- **Notes**

Psalm 100:4-5
Enter his gates with thanksgiving
and his courts with praise;
give thanks to him and praise his
name.
For the Lord is good and his love
endures forever;
his faithfulness continues through all
generations.

MY WEEKLY PRAYER

SCRIPTURE OF THE WEEK

PRAYER REQUEST

Week of: _____

Weekly Planner

This Week's Goal:

Important Tasks

Appointments

To Do List

Proverbs 16:9
The heart of man plans his way, but the Lord establishes his steps.

Weekly Goals

Day	Goals	Action Steps
Mon		
Tue		
Wed		
Thu		
Fri		
Sat		

GRATITUDE REMINDER

- **I am thankful for**

- **I am grateful for**

- **Notes**

Psalm 100:4-5
Enter his gates with thanksgiving
and his courts with praise;
give thanks to him and praise his
name.
For the Lord is good and his love
endures forever;
his faithfulness continues through all
generations.

MY WEEKLY PRAYER

SCRIPTURE OF THE WEEK

PRAYER REQUEST

Week of: _____

Weekly Planner

This Week's Goal:

Important Tasks

Appointments

To Do List

Proverbs 16:9
The heart of man plans his way, but the Lord
establishes his steps.

Weekly Goals

Day	Goals	Action Steps
Mon		
Tue		
Wed		
Thu		
Fri		
Sat		

GRATITUDE REMINDER

- **I am thankful for**

- **I am grateful for**

- **Notes**

Psalm 100:4-5
Enter his gates with thanksgiving
and his courts with praise;
give thanks to him and praise his
name.
For the Lord is good and his love
endures forever;
his faithfulness continues through all
generations.

MY WEEKLY PRAYER

_____

_____

_____

_____

_____

_____

_____

_____

_____

_____

_____

_____

_____

_____

SCRIPTURE OF THE WEEK

PRAYER REQUEST

_____

_____

_____

_____

_____

_____

_____

_____

_____

_____

_____

_____

_____

_____

_____

Week of: _____

Weekly Planner

This Week's Goal:

Important Tasks

Appointments

To Do List

Proverbs 16:9
The heart of man plans his way, but the Lord
establishes his steps.

259

Weekly Goals

Day	Goals	Action Steps
Mon		
Tue		
Wed		
Thu		
Fri		
Sat		

GRATITUDE REMINDER

- **I am thankful for**

- **I am grateful for**

- **Notes**

Psalm 100:4-5
Enter his gates with thanksgiving
and his courts with praise;
give thanks to him and praise his
name.
For the Lord is good and his love
endures forever;
his faithfulness continues through all
generations.

SCRIPTURE OF THE WEEK

PRAYER REQUEST

Personal Reflection

Month:

BAD HABITS I NEED TO STOP

THINGS I REGRETTED NOT DOING

THINGS I LEARNED THIS MONTH

HOW TO BE A BETTER VERSION OF ME

For I know the thoughts that I think toward you, says the LORD, thoughts of peace and not of evil, to give you a future and a hope.

Jeremiah 29:11

WHAT I LEARNED ABOUT MYSELF

THE GOOD HABITS I GAINED

WHY I LOVE ME!!!

NOTES

www.ingramcontent.com/pod-product-compliance
Lightning Source LLC
Chambersburg PA
CBHW080634030426
42336CB00018B/3192